Night Flying

Also by Roger Nash

Settlement in a School of Whales
Psalms from the Suburbs

Night Flying

Roger Nash

Goose Lane Editions

Published with the assistance of the Canada Council, 1990.

Some of these poems have appeared in *American Poetry Anthology*, *Antigonish Review*, *Arc*, *Ariel*, *Canadian Author and Bookman*, *Canadian Forum*, *Canadian Literature*, *Capilano Review*, *Challenging the Conventional*, *Contemporary Moral Issues*, *Dandelion*, *Malahat Review*, *Mirror Images*, *Muse Letter*, *Northward Journal*, *Poetry Canada Review*, *Prism international*, *Poetry Toronto*, *Quarry*, *Queen's Quarterly*, *University of Windsor Review*, *Wascana Review*, *Waves*, and *West Coast Review*.

"Night Flying" won First Prize in *Prism international*'s 1985-86 Poetry Contest. "To my wife of twenty years" received an award in the American Poetry Association's 1984-85 Annual Poetry Contest.

Book design by Julie Scriver
Cover art: "Untitled," pastel, by Pat Henderson, 1987
Printed in Canada by Centennial Print & Litho

Canadian Cataloguing in Publication Data

Nash, Roger 1942-
Night flying

Poems.
ISBN 0-86492-116-0

I . Title.
PS8577.A83N63 1990   C811'.54   C90-097548-2
PR9199.3.N37N63 1990

Goose Lane Editions
248 Brunswick Street,
Fredericton, New Brunswick
Canada E3B 1G9

for Chris

Contents

This Is My Mother's Camera

The Tea Ceremony

Trial by Ravens

Night Flying

Waiting and waiting for her in the park

The shadow of the sundial turns
a cogwheel in the sky.   Statues
stir and move their hands
above the lawn.   Flowerbeds
gently whir, then chime.
Her footsteps are late again,
until they come.   A red
dress is always on time.

Incident at London International Airport

Waiting in the mislaid lounge of the overdue terminal
for a delayed flight to Canada, our three-week-
old son, unswayed by such vain imaginings
as international datelines and difficulties with jet engines,
knowing only that the entire planet was suddenly
bitten with hunger under his own skin, began
lamentations for the end of all history.   With no alternative
in a jampacked airport, my wife put him to the breast
beneath her cape. This straightway produced a series of loud
clicking noises from our fellow travellers, as though
     they carried
small geiger counters in their hand baggage,
and we had released a harmful level of some activity that
     was lethal
to their lives.   Anyhow, our prospects of dealing peacefully
with our neighbours were declining alarmingly when, out
     of perfectly
thin air, which I had thought existed only
in stories, seven elderly ladies, dressed
all in black and bags of knitting, suddenly
surrounded us, smiling beatifically, as though
our son were every
grandson they ever had waited for, and they had just stepped
out of a fishing boat from the island of Cyprus
or Santorini, to greet his arrival and help organize
an immediate christening or circumcision, whichever
     mattered to them,

and one of them did.   Their elaborately lined faces somehow
let through a warming light, like frail parchments
lit from behind in a museum, and recording the lessons
of a lifetime of lives: that the hungry be fed, infants
and the weak protected, and the proud condemned to
    the discomfort
and clicking of their own lives. They formed a protective
wall around us, not even speaking, until my son fell
well asleep at the nipple.   When I looked up again,
    they simply
had vanished, within a second, leaving not even
a ball of wool or single plucked chicken behind.
And not a click could be heard throughout the whole
    terminal.

ice eggs

the ice hatched its eggs
into lakes of blue water,
and a flock of leaves clucked
on the birches in our back yard.
two small boys
ate the one last
mouthful of snow.   their smiles
flew up covered in mud.

Family discussion

My father often thinks of us since he
was dead.   Still dazed from the long-term
effects of his fatal heart attack,
he finds it hard to believe that our children
get born so undeservedly young, while he stays
slim and trimly defunct so late.

My father was completely fit until after
he died.   He allowed nothing to be wrong with him.
It was improper of the room to disappear so suddenly.
He put it down to a bomb attack.
He wants us to know we are wrong about something,
and that he, as usual, couldn't help being right.

It's the dead miss the living, and should be pitied.
For the living have grown the most arrogant and stiff.

On the stroke ward

Can you hear me, my mother?   Or are they my own
words streaming back, trying
to listen from your face?   Your eyes give out
a busy signal, or dial restlessly
around in the bed.   Lines are down
into the densely wooded interior, which draws
itself over rare birds of passage
you have never seen before.   Beneath
tall pines, a man in rags
is dying of complications from being my future
self.   He whispers a message I never
receive.   It wobbles a blade of grass.

If you can see me, blink your whole life
once.   If you cannot, blink the sun
through the window, but brightly, twice.   Are you here,
my mother?   Can you lean out of your eyebrows
to smile from your elbows up, and make me
in front?   Am I present, almost?   Your silence
draws a screen around me.   You seem perfectly alone
by myself.   I shall try to be the best
in you that can survive in myself.   I am staying
in a cloud for a while, moving rapidly
off out of the last familiar corner
of my eye, high above the Atlantic.

Can you move, my mother?   Even your name,
Margaret Ellen, can no longer turn
her lilting head to greet visitors
and flowers, and the window beyond, arriving
as a further tribute, full of vases
of weather and card after receding card
of blue, all invisibly signed
by the sun.   Is it language that's leaving that noise
in your throat?   Drafts rasp down the chimney.
They drown out shouts from a room that's impossibly
lost in a tower in the sky in a hospital
ward in the sea in this sootfall of verse.

Night flying

Each night, my grandmother prepared for flying
the piano, forty quick years ago.
Twin barrels were swivelled out
above the keyboard, and loaded with candles. Sandwiches
and bramble jam scones were stowed
in rows on the gleaming top of the instrument,
with a large reserve teapot, for use
in emergencies. Then the huge machine stood
poised and flickering in its hangar of firelight,
invisibly shifting weight up
its highly-strung legs, awaiting
the soft sooty clouds that drifted
away with our chimney.

           She would take her seat
briskly, without any ceremony, pushing
back black velvet cuffs
to an exact calibration that only she knew of.
The white lace collar was useful
for higher altitudes. When her fingers kneaded
the keys together, a motor spoke
deep in the mahogany, usually with Liszt's
Hungarian Rhapsodies, and piano, stool,
and my very own grandma rose fearlessly
above the distant fields of our Turkish carpet,
as I saluted stiffly in my sailor-boy
costume, and she floated out of the parlour
window, just clear of the rose
garden, lurching higher with each
crescendo, off behind the lines of every
enemy, as only grandmas can do.

She could land again only if I went straight
to bed and dreamed her a flat and sunny
field, with a sailor-suited boy
at the end of it.   Twenty years after her death,
she still comes in to land on occasion,
utterly unabashed at no longer being alive,
tugging down her cuffs and handing me a heaped
dream of hot jam scones.

The purpose of cats

When the sun isn't house-trained,
it leaves a yellow puddle
in each room.   Cats
sit in them, and accept the blame.

Surprises

Surprise is
a kitten being chased
by a large black
beetle; is
Wagner played
loudly, even under
the bathwater; is
a very tall
houseplant who looks like
Shakespeare; is
you, soaping my back
until it thinks my front
is new.

Night thoughts

When I crawl into bed to read one nightcap
of a poem, my wife hops lightly in beside me,
and watches two programmes at once on the T.V.,
alternating between them with the remote control button,
while she neatly completes a crossword puzzle in
   the newspaper,
using some other eye she keeps hidden for that purpose,
and rips pages of recipes she wants to file
from an old magazine, making a slow sound
like silkworms savaging mulberry leaves by an open
microphone, in between conducting several conversations
with girlfriends on the 'phone, about a garage sale,
   a workshop
for teachers, and, more interestingly, a submersible pump
   that can drive
water two hundred feet up somebody's cliff.
She has done all this, and has now been fast asleep
for over ten minutes.   The inactivity is deafening.
Quietness flails at me like a motorbike exalting itself
outside the only open window.   I can no longer
concentrate on reaching even the fifth line of the poem,
and begin to wonder whether reading literature is harmful
for one's versatility.   And, at three in the morning, I find
I've been worrying, awake or asleep, for over an hour,
about what size submersible pump it would take to propel
five lines of poetry clean through a bedroom.

I couldn't count the ways

I married a minnow and a tree once.
We were all very young, and I hadn't met you yet.
Now, though I can love whole forests
and hills in a glance, you are everywhere, unobtrusively,
even when you stay at home to avoid
the blackflies.   You have urged me on, after leaves
and young pebbles, unashamedly; and taught me
that the sky is however you feel, though its blue
is near to insatiable.   It is usually a journey
or adventure to see your face.   Without
you there, a pillow would be nothing.   I married you,
and there was no because; just warm and is, so close
that stars can brush between our toes.

The coppery weathercock

That bonfire blaze in the eye
from his twirling flight has spluttered
out.   Nets of frost
have snared him gray and still.
Now, who can hold us steady
by turning instead, as a tall
wind blows?   The street
veers uncertainly to the right,
quivering like the long black
needle of a faulty compass.
Inside, tea-cups rattle
and turn on their shelves, rapidly
losing all sense
of etiquette and direction.   We slide
together across the sofa,
and fall, by a fail-safe form
of gravity, well-tried after twenty
years of argument and marriage,
to land with a bump, far
in the back of each other's bobbing
eyes; finding there a warm
but gently wobbling spindle
for the day to turn around us.

To *my wife of twenty years*

I married you because your father appeared
in an interminable musical dream, and said:
Conduct her well, or I shan't stop.   Then your mother
flew by in an iron washtub, and whispered:
Make sure you wash with her once a week.

To be honest more slowly, I married you because
language could never be the same
without you beside me in it, making laughter
beneath that dreadfully untidy kitchen table,
so that words have something surprising to feel alive about.

I married the sea because its deepest
green surfaces constantly in your eyes;
so deep, it helps stars forget what grandmothers
they set sail under.   My name still frequently
forgets me when it sees you looking, and floats away.

I married you because our view of the hill
makes the windows astonished every day.   Is that
my life you're wearing tonight, with the neckline
that's interested in me?   If I were you, as I sometimes
am now, I would wear me more frequently.

Should I complain to the movers?

When they carted out the contents of our house,
they left empty rooms jampacked
with silence.   In the two fixed mirrors,
our reflections sank to a green light
at the bottom, and got overlooked.   Though my wife
   readjusted
the same hem and even higher hopes
as when we moved in, they didn't resurface.
Winters of talk round the fire still
gossiped themselves up the chimney.
They'd been trashed with the wind.

                              And this was where the lake
raised its wet muzzle to the windowsill,
to watch curious scenes of ourselves
through the eyes of a sensible otter.   Then an expansive
mood shivered over it, whatever it was
we were doing, and becalmed us too.
It would often watch us to forget myself.

When they shipped away our view of the lake
with the sofa, they ignored long lines
of language, reeling on down into wherever
there are deeps we may name after lakes, past
the daily ripples and catastrophes.   Look,
is that an otter, coming to bemuse us,
right at the windless edge of this page?
There are lakes to shimmer in any neck
of our words, as deep as we can speak our lives.

We are all of us amazing to be here

If my mother hadn't met my father, unpredictably
as is usual in these cases, under a clock-tower
and poplar trees that kept the time
too quickly, there would be no moon to fill
my night tonight.   There would be no night;
only something inadequately unlit that had never
enjoyed being deeply and resonantly dark.

If my father hadn't noticed my mother, on a day
whose birdsong can still be heard, passing
softly behind the colour of my eyes, and fading
in sunlight through the startled forest of my children's
hair, then, somewhere, inside an envelope,
inside a drawer, my best thoughts
and spectacles would, probably, have been mislaid by
    someone else.

If my mother hadn't talked to my father, the houses
we lived in around the world, and whole metropolises
of memories surrounding them, their cobblestones and horse
dung steaming intently at dawn,
to make sure the sun knew, would topple
into dust.   Then the dust would sift back
into something long before itself.

If my father hadn't walked with my mother, the ball
their grandsons play with in the park would never
have got kicked through the greenhouses of a cloud.
And I would still, impossibly, want to bequeath
to the two tall sons I had never had,
all the memories of swimming through the sunsets
of our lake that we were most fully incapable of.

Voyages of a garden shed

The shed had already returned from many voyages
when my brother and I signed on as crew, both
under six storms old.   Its door was invitingly
pockmarked with pellets from the airgun of an uncle
    who'd served
before us; though he'd spurned treacherous seas in a
    small orchard
for the safety of an army, and never returned.   Even
in light winds, that shed pitched and yawed
preposterously amid the plum trees.   From its one cracked
window, you could see the house disappearing beneath them
at times, yet always surviving, rising higher,
shrugging off even starlings on the uppermost branches,
standing as firm as a house could in those conditions.

We sailed in it carefully, for the seasons it visited were often
of its own invention, far off the beaten
track.   On sunny days, a grandfather might come
alongside to see us off, canvas billowing
from his deckchair.   He would blow smoke at us from his
    pipe, in the shape
of a floating but slowly dispersing guitar, which he insisted
on playing to us, chords wreathing after us as we rounded
the wall of the incinerator, headed for open seas
of heaving cherryblossom.   New continents drifted
into view across the fence.   We knew they were real,
for the shed

recalled them so uninterruptedly toward itself, having been
     to them all
but a shorter uncle or a longer somebody ago.

We had a struggle to keep our balance on the narrow deck,
with the hold always full of shifting sacks of extremely
damp onions, and an elderly bicycle that came
close to sprouting.   On those voyages, we discovered
     an eighth
day to the week.   It began when it wanted to, and just
took us along.   Once, we anchored by an island
where children were learning to feel no pain; though
     their shadows
still grazed far too easily, and bled
like rainbutts all over my brother's shirt.
He was never quiet or very asleep, but always
my brother.   The clouds were forgiving, and got used
     to seeing
the tops of our heads, as we dealt thoroughly with the ants.

Today, trying to fix my life in what seems
but a suppertime later, I find some of the same cargo
of unmistakably damp onions journeying beneath
     the kitchen
sink.   We recognize us all.   How little changed, for being
an ocean and sons of my own afar from the shed we once
set sail in.   I think I am ready to go again
on the longest of voyages.   Last night, the cloud

on my pillow drifted off unfamiliarly from the edge of
    the day.
As my wife bobbed encouragingly ahead in her red
flannel nightie, faint smoke from a grandfather's
guitar floated up from the fireplace.   Are you out
in the waters in front, and still always hungry, my brother?

The Mandarin of Morning

The mandarin of morning

When morning comes, we are always in China.
Joss sticks are lit somewhere out
on the lake, to make an offering of mist.   It flickers
with the swift brocades of ducks and herons.
Porcelain becomes a pale and unbroken sky.
In each breeze, water lilies
polish their ivories, and shuffle pieces
of a mahjong set.   Attentive beards
on the shore hold long pointed
leaves low.   Then the hills, officiating
only from far inside their silhouettes,
slowly unroll the scroll of a landscape
in the Sung dynasty.   Great fans
and parasols rustle overhead.   The mandarin of morning
has arrived again, with light lacquered to his feet.

Farming on water

The dipping prow
ploughs clouds
firmly under.
It rocks flocks
of birds into lengthening
furrows of flight.
At river bends,
oar blades
saw whole
reflections of trees
unevenly down,
opening up
clearings for larger
crops of blue.

Snaky lake

The island slides long granite
shadows into the lake.   They sink endlessly.
Deep water lies patiently
in wait from a thousand years ago.
It draws our canoe across the distant
sunless back of its mind, barely
noticing.   It is waiting for something more
important.   The paddle pokes a hole through,
meeting with no resistance, and has a bad
dream of falling noiselessly into a suddenly
dilated passive black pupil,
followed in on a slipstream by lost hills
and headlands;   all forgetting themselves in the dark
unwavering stare, hypnotized to the lake
bottom as skilfully as if by a snake.

Lake herding

officer i only look like a bum riding
this freight car but i once kept cattle
and several horses though im now a lake herder
first class yes sir nights
are the worst for lakes getting lost specially small ones
running splash bang into these brand new
unexpected highways slung right
across their ancient routes for roving so they dribble
    disconcertedly
away through the bushes swaying with cargoes of terrified
fishes signalling desperately across trees to each other
in that morse of flickering moonlight that none of them
    understand
some beach themselves hopelessly in the lobotomies of
    gravel pits
others flounder as far as main streets
and rose gardens surrounded by fire trucks
with injured sirens and the latest crop of high
pressure pumps to dismember their fluids muscle
by rippling muscle
                    im up every night calming them
coaxing them calling them back on course like a tide
of surging heifers for someones got to look after them
right across canada its a big job i can
tell you with a lot of travelling and no national
standards though we are the upstarts who confuse them
    laying
down malls and computer emporiums and expecting to
    find them

exactly in place the next morning when the whole wide
skin of the world twitches and switches about
each day as lively as the hide of an exquisitely immodestly
exuberant hog in the sun and its not only lakes
that go nomadic though thats my particular duty
mountains and valleys gallivant too yet more
patiently than us on a more relaxed schedule
mountains take millions of years ears
back sliding powerfully to their destinations
my pal six flat cars down hes
in charge of hills and mountains and no drunk
either but we need someone else for trees and grasses
for they fair rush about in overexcitement
we cant keep up with them would you care to join us

Lazarus raised in a canoe

As the paddle falls, lifts and falls,
it recovers slowly from the numbness of its wooden
limb: first a tingling in the blade,
a column of sonar hearing rising
through the haft; then knuckles straining the whites
of their rows of awakening eyes, both hands
absolved in the urgent forgiveness of new
senses eager to re-order their world.
Along the blade's edge, a curved lip
begins to sip thirstily under the water,
regaining an appetite.   It tastes at sudden
syrups from shallow inlets, and thick
molasses of mud from muskegs, that soothe
down the river's throat.   A strange awareness
flutters into place between the shoulder-blades,
muscles dreaming, in colour, of the birth
of sprinting waves.   The paddle, alert
in its life, sideslips, then soars unerringly
among updrafts from rapids that heave eagles
nearly higher than their flight.   The canoe
leaps up onto sheer mist and sunshine,
riding, at last, its wingspan of spray.

Losing our shadows

Out on the lake, two years ago,
our shadows paddled effortlessly across the surface
of this rock, three inseparably in a row.
They turned to us and waved, so that we,
in accordance with the perpetual laws of navigation,
waved vigorously back.   For a moment,
those shadows, creased and grained with the urge
of glaciers and quartz, became as lasting as the rock
itself.   They cast our canoe casually by,
and us fleetingly out into our lives
on the fidgeting lake, limbs effervescing
with the short season of sunlight, sensations
of wind as sudden and as frail as dragonflies.
Today, we find only two of the shadows
on the rock.   Yours, my mother, can no longer
cast you accurately back into your empty
seat in the day, making, as is proper,
not a single splash or wobble.   It has floated
far behind the lichen on the rock, overlapping
with shadows of other wayfarers from the past
in a composite silhouette, drifting enduringly
back into the unhurried crystals of granite,
probably all of you still waving.

At the edges

At the edges of ponds, a fine froth
embroiders its beetles among unfailing reflections
of clouds—and the wheels of lost bicycles.
The pattern is sumptuous.   How else could earth
and sky hold everything together?

At the margins of sight, something always
steps sideways, a hill or even a snake.
Then it waits for the turn of a head.   Eyes
can't come to the brink of this world by tumbling off,
cornea whirling, and nowhere to get a grip.

At its trembling corners, a light voice
calling from the far field fades
into pure sunlight.   Her soft lips
pour past the hills in a high shining.
Each bright day brings her back.

At the fringes of one life, someone
slips into the centre of another.   Beetles
scoot lazily out from the brim
of the pond, and sail by with clouds.   They flip
back their legs, and ride among bicycles.

Chair at the dump

Outlines worn
in the corduroy of this chair
insist on reseating
the lives that sagged
right through them.   Springs
stir expectantly,
as wind knocks
at the cloud of yet another
long-awaited
door.   Absent
elbows shine,
and leak rain
and abandoned horsehair
everywhere.

Evening

Evening draws the calm
of grandmothers about us, darkening its blues
to a lavender-scented shawl.
Small birds are embroidered
into the elaborate quietness of their nests.
At the hem, a fringe of fieldgrass
wavers shyly against the unploughed
outlines of sleep.   Everything
is held by a modest brooch
of the most understated of stars.

This Is My Mother's Camera

Is there still plenty of paper?

Somewhere, a poem was born
so that I could get written.
I hunt for it, week by day
by each sprouting line.   I think
I may almost have reached a first
crumpled draft, in pencil
and a slightly greying beard.
I have on my old torn coat.
Is there still plenty of paper?

Please write to me in this poem

I am reading this poem only
for you to want to write it
to me.   Then our lives can try
to meet by whatever window
you choose to sit near.
Are you ready?   I will open these spaces
for you to lean your words into.

....

....

....

But please write louder.
Your face is not coming
through very clearly.   Wait.
I can hear the hazel green
of your eyes almost forming, should they have
that colour.   Or are they still mine,
out looking for you?
If you don't reach me at first,
please try again
later, on this or another
piece of paper.   Hello?

Photo of an angry man

This man is so angry,
he was already dead.
His skin-tight smile
pulls on the trigger,
as he aims the barrels
of both loaded
eyes straight
at the camera.   He shoots himself
in the centre of our looking
at his life.   All
the photos in the album
are loosened by the blast.

Abstract art

I am a painting
looking at you.   And what
are you a person about?
Is your well-drawn
face of a bumpy
potato?   Your hands
of a nervous cat?
You should shape your life
into something you communicate.
Else what sense can you make of us?

On Chagall's "The Falling Angel"

When we clamber upwards in men's eyes,
up on the lacquered rungs of praise,
grant us the natural grace to trip,
and, lunging outwards, fall.   For blessed
are they who topple to their true ascent.
May we tumble up into the downward
rising sound of your name, gathering
radiance like meteors in the friction of your invisible
hand.   Enable us to fall as high
as any moon, descending far above
the rinse of time;   time falling too,
grandfather clocks twisting in our wakes,
hands fluttering at ten to two.
Blessed are they who can stoop to hear
the candleflame's quiet, though stormclouds
pour the very vilest of their inks.
May their candlesticks be always green.
May the lights in their eyes go unflickering.
Humble us into the highest of high places,
floating in a buried sky above Vitebsk.

The new bank building

Each dawn, our new bank building
hangs the multi-storied mirrors
of its walls beneath a passing cloud, and presents
permanently-sealed windows as open
for their usual business.   Every acre of glass
is bright and insatiable, collecting reflections
from the town.   They take in everything that happens.
Nothing is too large or too small for their prompt
attention.   The day's first bus
is deposited instantly, with a deft flex
of quicksilver, onto the shutters at the second floor,
along with a protesting bag-lady.   In mere
micro-seconds, the entire town has been transferred
impeccably.   But what is there left for a mirror
this accomplished to do?   Neighbouring windows,
hustling for new custom, start
to eye and plunder each other with shining efficiency.
On Mondays, having pegged up rows of wet
clouds from the backyards opposite, they miraculously
multiply the same pair of red
longjohns into the long deep streak
of a perpetual sunrise.   Sleepy pedestrians
shiver in the early morning air,
uncertain, despite several cups
of coffee, whose reflections they are;
legs shattering into slivers of glass
as they stumble on potholes that city council
has already denied are really there.

An *old family recipe*

"How to make nothing happen."   This was my
    grandmother's recipe.
It won't mind me sharing her with you in whatever kitchen
    you call
your life.   There is room for us, if you read by the
    window.   See,
we are arriving already.   It will make us a marvellous lunch.

Take a sky as vaporously blue as its own
reflection in a saucer of milk.   Don't let
the cat sip it, though sparrows may.   Listen, until trees
throw back their shoulders, and breathe vigorously into
    your day.

If you are fortunate, nothing at all will begin to happen.
Clouds can forget everything we never needed to learn.
One flowerpot on the lawn will know anything
that's important.   It makes you and the rain shine.

On the retirement of a Professor of English

After a lifetime of reading, I have learned to be at a loss
to know, what, don't tell me, let me
think; or, better, to settle for an off-shore
gust tugging again at my back, as I turn
the pages to let them breeze right
through my life.   It is hard to remember that my books
were once sealed with many seals; and the seals
themselves had seals set upon them,
often with depictions of strenuous voyages
over moving depths of water, with only
the faintest whiff of islands in between.

The first key that turned me swung me
open on courtyards that were completely bare.
One could sit in the shade and breathe, what-
is-it, the distant, something, was it, orange blossom,
and wonder why one had entered at all.
Later, one stumbled on courtyards within that courtyard,
full of the sound of fountains with further
fountains playing within them, and eventually out
onto a street that swayed with countless readers
hurrying to the heart of the, place where we, there,
wherever we knew we'd find we'd been going
all along.

As you stepped into that dusty cloud
of travellers, you heard coughs and other curious
rumours about the, somewhere: where lives the apothecary
with salves that heal all wounds;
in what rooms the best of stories relate
the lives of their tellers, without mercy or evasion,

before rapt audiences; in what temples the gods
still faithfully pray for a human race
to at least half-believe in them.   When you arrived
in the market-place, there were feastings of words, often
roasted on spits that spluttered and ran
with the fat of gutturals, as glistening as duck
or mutton.

       Bit by bit, you learn
to thread your way through the maze of thoroughfares
that become as familiar as dreams were always
welcome; as much part of your nature as, who were they,
names that come to live on the tips of the tips
of our tongues.   At some point, among frequent donkey
droppings and the smell of open drains,
one has gone too far to turn
back and imagine seals on books again.
More sailors arrive in the harbour each day,
shirts fluttering like wild-fire behind them.
They have far eyes, or beards who can smile at them.

We are now climbing the cobblestone lanes
as they wind up the hillside, travelling deeper
through memory.   The air is turning to wine.
Statues have started to wave their hands about,
beckoning the horizon.   Somehow, home
is across and over our shoulders, listening
for us from where clouds blow out of the very beginning
of language, streaming away on all sides.
Soon we will be speaking to you from inside the weather.
Tomorrow, what sun will make our day into?

A rare gramophone recording: my father-in-law
the conductor

The needle skates out from the edge
of a frozen black pond.   Its glittering
path levers into the afternoon sun
the waterlogged voices of a choir that's forgotten
it sang.   Among the bulrushes, a flock of agitated
coughs have robustly outflown their audience.
Then, almost lost at the bottom, comes
the quick eel of a conductor's baton,
surfacing suddenly with an electrical reef
of unbelievably red Welsh hair.
Even the surface clattering and hiss
can be transformed in a moment, through the subtle
    technologies
of memory and affection, into a part of his life:
the low rumble of furniture vans
that he rehearsed carefully toward new homes,
only part-time and out of season,
supporting the fragile poetry of marriages
with the enduring patronage of music; whistling
reliably to keep the engine going;
folding his flat cap practically,
to keep out damp or unwed
weather; driving exuberantly, though he always
suspected it, toward this distant black pool
that has become his last and well-labelled address.
He commands me, throughout the crescendos, to perform
    and cherish
his youngest daughter, as I was wise enough
fool to marry her; telling me, records
often listen to the lives that play them,
though we get horribly out of tune.

This is my mother's camera

Which I am given since plants in her garden
knew the least significant of our names
when we walked there together, and made us feel
we had a place among the look of things.
A window informs me there's a film inside
already, with five shots taken.
Your mistress's eyes have laid you down
at last, slid slowly away
from the five sights, as yet unknown to me,
stored in the clever chemistry of your dark;
the film, like any life, left
surprisingly unfinished.   Your spooling memory
awaits nineteen more snapshots
from her life, screwed face lined
up to the apparatus with the enormity of the task,
and days taking on a shutter speed
her legs could not keep up with.
Should I finish the film?   And whose album
will I paste my life into?   I point the camera
aimlessly, and the lens of this poem's language
suddenly adjusts, revealing you,
crouched in the boat, as you did on your visit
two years ago, still waiting
for that perfect shot of a heron.   I try
to whisper through the lens that it's there, to the right,
posing magnificently.   But I can't communicate
with you in your last nineteen shots.   I can only
hold the camera steady, so that the lake
and trees won't rock or spill a single
drop.   You turn your head and look
right though me, snapping furiously.   You have got
the shots you were waiting for, and leave me with something
blue and flying upwards in my life.

The Tea Ceremony

Uncle Lennie's third proof of the existence of a question

In the beginning was a voice.   But no-one
can remember precisely what words
it was saying.   There is still disagreement.
Yet we're as sure as pickled eggs
that it was singing.   From the rise in the chant,
it was likely singing a question.
So the orderly sequence of stars,
this succession of roof tops and children,
the stream of autos gleaming
from the plant, are bound together
only by the asking of a very
strong question, eh?

Deep-water fugue

Whales and hump-backed church organs
call to each other across the sound.
Beneath the flat surface of stacked Bibles
and calmed memorial tiles,
a ponderous movement limbers up
at a steady two knots,
cracked leather lungs wheezing
softly, rising buoyantly
on a pedalled stream of air.   The steeple
hums like an expectant mast.
Arches in the nave curve their stone
sails.   A long oily
note surfaces abruptly, sides
awash with sounds, pouring off
torrents of sheer glissandos, silvery
with small fry of deep-water
flutes, sparkling with sheets and loud
points of lightening, whole
icicled riggings.   The horizon heaves-ho
outside stained-glass windows,
purpled trees billowing expectantly,
waiting for the town to turn
on its tide, and ebb back to the beach,
street by barnacled street.
Large organ pipes bask
expansively in each other's identities.
Their calls sweep down the aisle like a sonar;
and, out past the door,
stun cyclists, sparrows and swerving
clouds without unfair distinction.

Now the great fugue arches its back
and accelerates.   A solid square
forehead of sound thrusts up
to the rafters for a final blow.
Then, lifting the tall tail fin
of its vanishing coda, it sinks away,
carrying after it a wake of mildewed
raincoats bobbing on the backs
of startled congregants, adrift in their seats.

May the great blue and rare
beaked organs never be silent
in our waters; or the double-stopped steep
dives of dolphins down the sides of cathedrals.

Double burial under glass (Dorchester museum)

Your Bronze Age burial is boldly
labelled beneath the glass top of our lives.
After centuries of moving in marriages under the moss,
sinking solemnly as dolphins down
from the last green light, trailing
groves that still smoke with mists that linger
from your sight, you have become the third exhibit
past the ticket booth and toilet door.
The land you were hauled from was long since
stamped out; rivers left
without lustre from your drinking faces.   Your roads
were settled by hillslopes of dust, travelling
in their own inimical directions.   Names
on maps still talk about your huts and journeys.
They never give up trying
to utter you back into place at dawn,
on a sodden track to the river, oxen
and beech trees shaking shaggily
under rain, soluble spirits streaming
from rocks to the river, puddles worked
well with the copper mines of stars.
It is a stubborn trait in a language, to try
to revive its speakers against such odds.

Bones braided tightly together,
fused by the underground surgery of minerals
and dark, your embrace of each other is as inscrutably
private as the cloudiest glimmer of quartz.
It is unbreakable, and excludes everything perfectly.
We would-be voyeurs through the glass-topped
cabinet of history are not protected by hermetic
seals on the glass.   Your embrace slowly

omits us from the room.   Our words jig
in midair with the cigarette smoke, struggling
to drag us back by the short words
of our vocabularies ("D'you think they screwed like us?").
But our meanings are less muscular than theirs, unfit.
We are winnowed from where we stood.   Outside, in the
   carpark,
the dusts keep on travelling in their own
directions, and none of our maps fit.

Vespers

When our church's completely automated carillon
beams its evening praise into every
cranny of the town, a new and faultlessly
invisible organist seizes us in the computerized
absence of his hands.   Birds in the park
fall silent, and take a break
to retape their sessions.   Clouds stop
frolicking over the spire.   They slide by on an orderly
conveyor-belt of blue.   Couples
at the counsellor's let their perfectly pre-programmed
mouths say everything for them.   In the fields,
lines of harvesting machines lay
bare the bowed skulls of rabbits,
in observance of the last of the light.   And, in the bar,
brightly-lit theologues turn
to speculating whom God can pray to, to be forgiven
a growing sense of emptiness and loss.

Women at windows

Women at windows, women looking
from windows, looking from upper chambers
out over green and blue years
that count waves to their strangled hair.
Waiting as completely as fields distorted
by birds.   A fox of time howls
furtively into their bones.   Waiting for the sea
to winch up its wrecks; rebuild
with hammers of headlands and long nails
hidden in bays; return men
and boys, freshly on furlough from bustling
shipyards of sunbeams in water, dressed
and rested in double-breasted raiment of spray.

Windows in women, windows opening
in women, opening from clock-filled
walled-in sighs.   Listening for guns
to recall their pretty puffs of smoke,
magazines to clip back their bullets
in mint condition, shiny helmets
to fly back out of the dust
and rejoin their newly unwounded heads,
memory to remember itself, to roll back
a little from the left, savouring a world
that is suddenly seen again, long udders
of clouds nourishing the shell-holes
into nests of birds, and trees to learn from them.

Women become windows, women whose hands
become windows, skin worn bleary
and clear at the fingers, watering like glass.
Framing glimpse after glimpse at their knuckles
of a white as bloodless as apple blossoms

in the gardens of their youth.   Spring and skies
float by their thin and uncurtained palms
and shine palely though them.   Waiting

for faded family groups beneath the trees
to return to the camera, greet and regroup
on the darkness of film, and leave by the broken
lens to make a completely different,
yet no better, start on things.

A *dream*

A beggar in Cairo once proudly offered
me change.   The street was paved with sores
and his name.   Now he returns in the penniless
logic of a dream, eyes as wide
and green as minarets.   In the background, a camel
speaks every language simultaneously.
As before, I misunderstand each one perfectly.
The yellow mouth fondles its wobbling
hand-held teeth.   It is trying to tell me
my name, which escapes me.   But I feel flies
tickling blood out of who-is-it's veins.

In an abandoned country churchyard

Light shines on their names.   Frail stones
crumble as surely as cheese in the flurry of seasons,
a strong wind chiselling into them from the future.
Lines have unwritten that they ever were lived.   Light
shines on the revisions.   Rain falls once more,
having failed to remember it fell just yesterday for almost
a century.   Light shines on the rain.   Starlings
in the church tower start their song again,
which for them can be neither remembered nor forgotten.
It comes with the daylight just the same.   Light
shines through their song.   The sun swings slowly
on its cracked and unheard bell, shimmering a golden
silence over the churchyard, smoothing out
any rough edges remaining on the stones.
Could some last sharp trumpet ever carve
its message through here?   Light shines effacingly
on my question.   The starlings suddenly wheel and
      pronounce
on me a vigorous and most ungolden aerial benediction.
It fills in the lettering on some of the stones.   Light
shines on the vigour of their returning green names.

The tea ceremony

In the room of her memory, where tea was always,
but it was ALWAYS, taken, a fuse blows.
Her long-dead father looks startled.   Cups
rattle, and his face leaves.   In her ears,
years of rumours from villages dismantle
down to their smallest components, no more audible
than the siftings of sugar in her slightly dented
silver sugar bowl.   Voices
unscrew into slender peepings of frogs.
They hop gently away, beyond
the last windows.   Her fingers slowly
slough off the soft skin of sensations,
as patiently as a snake.   The feel of her feathery
nightdress comes away in her hand like a brass
doorknob.   Her echoes fall asleep
in the wall.   Bricks age, and crumble
awake to the peepings of frogs, who demand
new swamps in the villages, since tea
must, but it MUST, be taken in rooms
where fathers still try to fix the dampened
fuses, and someone else's cup
of memories begins to fill, with its three
sugars or two rumours again.

Cleaning the brasses

The day after Friday was for cleaning the church brasses.
My two maiden aunts, who seemed to scent even their
    names,
Dorothy with soap, Muriel in a streamlet of lavender
water, took me with them.   They let me help by watching
    them.
When they unfolded their cloths from the basket, metal
    polish
reeked out as suddenly and as strong as God's
own armpit, wafting up the aisle.
Elbows pushed and prodded with the patience of pistons,
until the collection plate grudgingly handed back their thin
reflections, lopsided and wobbling a bit from a week's
nonexistence.   My aunts abstemiously shared a single
small smile, and their greying hair grew
golden and magnificent, as I knew they were.   At last,
the empty candlesticks burst into flames again, flickering
beneath their blackened fingers, but carefully consuming
    nothing.
And when my aunts spoke, their voices came out
of something so suddenly shining, I could no longer see
    them.
They were no longer there.   Afterwards, they reappeared
    unobtrusively,
drinking tea from a thermos in the organ loft,
with no explanation of where they had been, matter-of-factly
readjusting their hat-pins and rolling down their sleeves.

Now, many years after, when they have both
gone behind the panelling of the organ loft forever,
as knowingly in the end as mice, I realize they are the only
saints I have ever yet seen, and what it is they have taught
    me.
The ice on our lake melts, with waves giving back
somewhat straighter reflections of our lopsided lives.
And my wife
burns in my arms once more, with no forewarning,
no smiles in triplicate, yet lovingly consuming nothing.
Who knows when what we've dulled may, astonishingly,
return to its shine?

Trial by Ravens

The shaking

All the walls went hoarse in the hubbub.   Bombers
were returning home from around the world, eager
for demobilization.   Rank after rank
of them clambered down through a tousled roaring in
     the trees,
the clouds in their cockpits still full
of the stench of lightening.   Grown-ups danced
in the street, and, afterwards, in the fronts of each other's
eyes.   Was it only the smallest of us kids
who saw how that deep and ceaseless rumbling overhead
drove ripples across the ponds like long
spiked nails?   Even girls' dresses
never stopped shivering around them.   Half
a century of soot haemorrhaged down just
swept chimneys.   It seemed hearths would never
heal.   And crayons left on the table
overnight had by morning scribbled a view
from your life that made everything look as thin
and as tangled as string.   It was clear that something
had shaken loose in the homecoming that would not be
tightened easily again.   From inside my grandpa's
banjo case, leant against the wall,
came the faint sound of strings
being stirred by a stealthy hand, and, endlessly,
an uneven music playing, playing.

Note found in the insane asylum

When I walked on water, I was charged
with a marine violation.   When I stood
still, they arrested me for constituting
a deep-sea obstacle.   When I multiplied
fishes down at the market,
the bottom fell out
of sales, animal rights
groups lodged an appeal,
and the bakers grew nervous
and formed their pickets.   When I calmed
the waters of Lake Superior,
scientists sued me for disrespect
of the laws of nature; and weatherforecasters
invited me to join their union.
When I raised armies from the dead,
both Russia and America accused me
of having defected to the other side
with their most secret weapon.
When I turned whisky into water,
I was fined for industrial sabotage.
When I spoke at my funeral, they searched
for the hidden tape-recorder.
So I got up and left, to start again
in Winnipeg.   But the coroner stopped me,
for unhygienic disposal of human
remains; and my Insurance Company
filed proceedings for fraudulent
intent on my life insurance.
My psychiatrist says I dreamed
all this, and no-one will read it.
So, why are you reading it?

Message transmitted from a distant constellation

Our world is a world
of great winds ranging over continents
in herds, rogue ears held
aloft, straddling fig trees
impetuously, mating moistly with mountains,
yet side-stepping cobwebs out of ancient respect.

This world is a world
where shafts of sunlight smoke into the oceans,
where ceaseless tongues stir up a cloud
of dust, where bent pillars of sulphur
lean above our cities, though a lingering scent
on the sheets at dawn still smells of grass.

This world, our world,
brings reprieves to the just executed,
inheritances to the yet unconceived, rebirth
to dawns and small stones, but extraditions
to whole continents.   The lips of our youngest
children taste continually of storms.

This world, as a world,
was always too large or too
small to know how to live on; its sunsets
too sudden to distribute fairly.
We frequently fought for a share of the clouds
and soft blouses for our women in summer.

Our world is a world
where youth always, surprisingly, ended.
Morning mist faded indiscernibly

for centuries.   It was stored at the backs of our ancestors'
eyes.   Each world has songs that won't ever
be sung, and its haze of vaporized pianos.

On our one world,
we are wearing our best for this special transmission.
Shoes no longer quite fit.   We kiss you
across time on whatever you count as your lips.
Please don't bother to answer this.   Disinfect
our words by rinsing them twice in your music.

The world's last poem

The world's
  last
  poem
will show
  what
  is
  left.

The world's
  last
  poem
will show
the world's
  last
  poem.

This is
the world's
  last
  poem.

Poem : meoP

One day

One day, out of a naive blue sky,
the swooping hawk will be denied its prey;
herons placed forever in the safety
of their own lost shadows.   The lion
will seethe by the still unclawed lamb.

Salmon at mid-leap will poise perpetually,
netted in a sun-like glint from their scales,
unable to regain the longed-for ledge
of their now boiling waterfall.   Even rocks by the river
will ignite as readily as ever the dew.

On the maternity ward, frail lungs
will fill with the miraculous fire of their first
cry; and proud fathers reach,
with interminable slow-motion, into evaporated
pockets for already consumed cigars.

In churches, "I do's" will echo among the remaining
arches, as brides and grooms precede
their vows into a nuptial silence, escaping
the tin cans tied to their melting cars
without even slipping through the fused side doors.

And murderers will be saved from the noose after the last
moment for pardons, fleeing through fiery
trapdoors, masks gone from their lit-up
faces, waiting, without any more time,
for the forgiveness of floors to rush up and greet them.

Trying to think of the unthinkable

Talk of megatons and range of missiles slips through
thought's short fingers, which have trouble even counting
out change at the store for a carton of eggs.   For a species
which always had problems accepting the death of its
    parents,
estimates of the end of a race sound like unbelievable
entries in an unavailable book of records, equivalent,
perhaps, to the entire population of New York
getting itself shot in a single 'phone booth.
Warned of a planet inherited, at best, by mutating
tribes of insects, we deviously begin to daydream ourselves
into somehow still standing comfortably there, viewing
flattened farms and factories, while filled to the brim
with a not unpleasant sadness at the harsh lives
of our predecessors, their efforts graced now by the spread
of wild rose and eager crabgrass.   In this insect
world, there will be plenty of fine ruins for us to feel
nostalgic about.   Yet crabgrass and wild rose
will be cindered, a thick dust standing in the air.
This is all that will be seen of nature's emblems of how
    humans
once lived: showing us, were we still there,
that love is inconceivable now as like anything else
but a red, red dust, dribbling down through the air.

Homo neanderthalensis

You gained power, over so many centuries
of absence from the earth, to have warred and loved
far less selfishly than us.   Heavyset on hilltops,
wherever you are again and again unseen,
absolute extinction enables you to pursue
an alternate lack of destiny, unhindered
by our terminal thoughtlessness.   On the banks
  of blackened
rivers, you can watch our immense improbability.
Shadows leach out from under our feet
in each bitter rain.   Alive, you won
your lack of point.   Extinct, you wait
on ours at night, from just beyond the wobbling
firelight, eager to touch huge
but gentle hands with us, that tremble with their massive
need of strength.   You, who clutched
clumps of yarrow and cornflower, thistle
and groundsel, hyacinth and marrow, plaiting them
in patterns on your dead in the Shanidar cave
just sixty-thousand brief blossoms ago,
will you bring shadows of your flowers to decorate us,
white and yellow, red and the shadow
of blue, when our species' time comes?

Trial by ravens

Only ever half-glimpsed, through some quick chink
between branches, a shrinking keyhole of dark
and draughty consciousness, skin prickling
right to the back of your eyes, the ravens
are aroused and in session again in the next unlit
clearing of the forest's lengthening memory.
Earnest in black, at ease in their catastrophic
cackling, caw, straw, pitch
black guffaw, the air around them getting
thicker with slapping waves then solid
walls of stink, something damp
is smeared on their feathers, and a limp stench
laid in their midst, no longer covered
by its skin.   Hot beaks furred,
some strange power zips in electrical
glistening ink along their backs, wings
conducting it, forking it, flinging it forward
in quick jerks, beaks jabbing
down and out.   The leafmould, patient
as usual, lies moist and loosely
clawed to lick it up.   The ravens
are gathered in court to conduct trials
and executions on behalf of the earth.   They judge
clouds free to go.   Trees
and limestone, dripping with the anticipation, must stay.
The whole forest stirs and drops
judgement and loose branches upon itself.
Will we be permitted to walk by for today, until the next
unexpected time and clearing?   Wings
hang over us in the pine trees.   They are considering it.